Love and Its Derangements

Love and Its Derangements

Poems by

JOYCE CAROL OATES

LOUISIANA STATE UNIVERSITY PRESS

Baton Rouge

A number of the poems published here have appeared previously
in the following periodicals: *Beloit Poetry Journal, Black Moss,
Carleton Miscellany, Carolina Quarterly, Chelsea Review, Colorado
State Review, Connexion, Denver Quarterly, Epoch, Epos, Fiddle-
head, Literary Review, The Little Magazine, McCall's, Malahat Re-
view, Michigan Quarterly, Orange Bear Reader, Pebble, Prism
International, Quarry, Saturday Review, Southern Review, Southern
Humanities Review, Southwest Review, Tamarack Review, Trans-
atlantic Review, Tri-Quarterly Review,* and *Western Humanities
Review.* To all these, acknowledgment and thanks are due, as well as
to the Albondocani Press, which published a different version of one
of these poems in *Women in Love and Other Poems,* 1968.

ISBN 0–8071–0847–2
Library of Congress Catalog Card Number 75–122357
Copyright © 1970 by Joyce Carol Oates
All rights reserved
Manufactured in the United States of America by
Kingsport Press, Inc., Kingsport, Tennessee.
Designed by Jules B. McKee

To my husband, Raymond

Passion is the element in which we live; without it, we hardly even vegetate. —BYRON

Contents

Love and Its Derangements

Parachuting

O our clothes buckle
crazily about our thighs
the wind screams bright and sharp
as castanets
or summer insects
everything flashes upward!
like roosters' feathers

together we fall down a highway
of steep air
the air is unbuttoning itself wildly
and love bursts

my love you are bursting
inside me   your atoms hot like coins
or cinders
why is the sky streaking upward?
why are we such heavy weights?

we are public here like roosters'
red fighting feathers
climbing the barnyard in fight
dirty and loving in air
scrambling red combs and toenails
their blood flecking happily outward
to arc upon the barnyard dust
to dots that dry shaped
like cindered stars

it is a scramble of lights and screams
like insects' deaths
two heavy weights falling amorous of earth
falling to flatten breasts and bellies
finally against the earth

Sleeping Together

nothing approaches
   the room's corners are backed out of sight
    nothing is inscribed on the eyelid's underside
    nothing strains for a voice

the whitest hollows of the body
   are gently cleft by shadows
    out of short damp curls
     the knuckles of two backbones stretch
      the length of an ordinary bed

light arrives slowly
   womanly upon skin
    the lashes of our eyes ring fatal targets
     lava of flesh flowing to one level
      we sleep together in two bodies
       our eyeballs still curved blind in skulls

lungs: warm sacs love-warmed
   hips rocked by waves of sleep
    we think together in thoughts like waves
    unsurfacing
     the dimensions of ordinary sound are lost
      in the smooth ridges of the body
       in this lazy magnifying light

already like ashes
   perfumed, our bodies surrender
    souls ground finely like spices
    like ashes
     sifted together in breaths like sand
      like ashes helpless after death
       hands and forearms grip loosely
        the perfect bones gripping beneath the flesh

such dimensions are lost in sleep
　in this lazy magnifying light
　　it is infinite
　　　in infinite light our bodies are lost

"Only the Exhaustive Can Be Truly Interesting"
—Thomas Mann

now you are crossing rooms
you are part of a new dimension

back here you are interpreted
in my body
held as in a reed, suspended
a moment walled-up and suspended

the flash of iridescent wings
turned to powder
on a man's thumb—
which may be used for crucial
identification—

is our affection
to be dragged everywhere today?

sanctified are trailer trucks hauling
matter across my vision, as are
the rooms you cross endlessly

men cross and recross rooms
women contemplate their bodies
silent and baffled as bandages
and white with the body's
tainted white

separated now
by half a daytime city
I contemplate you in
myself
in the tributaries of my
darkest body

6

About me
the time turns articulate again
dumbness passes as it must
into wit
the sirens of our bodies dissolve . . .
betrayed while the afternoon
moves on locked in the perpetual
shape of a library's
clock

Turning into Another Person

the tide of his veins
is stronger than mine
osmotic, the din of his
thoughts rises

his dreams wander like flames
the small complete faces
of his childhood
have the authority of faces
hacked out of wood

our invisible and visible hairs
merge
clear as nails

like peas popping ripe
dried out of their encasements
his parents' strange notions
overcome mine

turning into another person
we have the look
of living
of beginning again
in a new latitude

we have the look
of being complete

The Grave Dwellers

Geometry created us.
Perfect of proportion, we love
in rooms; doors chaste
as blank foreheads open
to our private keys.

The body is a muscle
to be regarded.
The brain is a muscle
of busy hills, the struggle
of unthought things with things
eternally thought.

Outside our rooms are
fences that sink into the earth:
roots curling in that darkness
are cut in pieces, unliving.
Our earth is filled in with
broken bricks, boards,
and old nails.

In a box we maneuver
from a set of walls
to another set of walls—
no space in between.
Our stories, told quickly,
are symbols of ourselves, the people
we must be, the lovers, inspired
to an infinite love
in a series of boxes.

"Woman Is the Death of the Soul"

fathoms deep with anger
wind and sun in a perpetual convulsion
of the evil dead

    a white flower along a branch
    a spirit sleeping in a tree
    women imagine music, sleeping
    dreaming along a branch, in sheerest light

womanly, death is an opening of cracks
small as threads, a tender failure of verbs,
the glossy male precision of the eye
gone permanently white

men with their passion pass
into me, and forget their precise
shapes

    their angry souls, freed,
    have no more meaning, or the meaning
    of wind and sun and air
    with their masculine haste, forever
    moving across the earth—

Loving

A balloon of gauze around us,
sheerest gauze: it is a balloon of skin
around us, fine light-riddled skin,
invisible.

If we reach out to pinch its walls it floats from us—
it eludes us wetly, this sac.

It is warmed by a network of veins
fine as hairs and invisible.
The veins pulsate and expand to the width
of eyelashes.
In them blood floats weightless as color.
The warm walls sink upon us when we love
each other, and are blinded by the heavier skin
that closes over our eyes.

We are in here together.
Outside, people are walking in a landscape—
it is a city landscape, it is theirs.
Their shouts and laughter come to us in broken sounds.
Their strides take them everywhere in daylight.
If they turn suddenly toward us we draw back—
the skin shudders wetly, finely—
will we be torn into two people?

The balloon will grow up around us again
as if breathed out of us, moist and sticky and light
as skin, more perfect than our own skin,
invisible.

Duet

I am looking at our hands.

These fingers are confusing, so many
of them. There is something sad about them,
tamed and lightly paralyzed fingers.

In the beginning our fingers
cut one another clean to the antiseptic bone.
They struck and cleaved and were parallel
of thought. Squeezing my hand you squeezed
the nail into the flesh—
all that has healed.

Is this the sequence the score demands?
The double movement completing an adagio duet,
the difficult turns, spins, feats of lifting
being over.

Traveling with You

all day the naked soil passes
the outline of the mountains is blunt
baked in hot staring light

the radio keeps losing itself
in unfamiliar air

we speak and are silent and the sun is immersed
in the moisture of sudden clouds
the moisture reflects heat in singular drops
eternally

"The day is so beautiful," we say to ourselves
and we think of the West which is eternal
and wider than ourselves and more silent

the wind has made ragged the leaves of such trees
as exist out here
their trunks are shredded and raw
they have no fruit to fall rotten to the ground
only rocks that kneel heavy with adoration

is this an enchanted land, so lovely?

we argue and are silent and forgive each other
the radio is adjusted to a song of raspy love
not so wide and silent as this land
"The sunset is so beautiful," we say to ourselves
in our human language which is a kind of silence
and the words drift in fear into silence
into enchantment

our suitcases are piled neat in the backseat of the car
the shampoo and mouthwash and cologne not upset
the radio's red needle can be adjusted
to contain all human language

15

the music is sprightly and neat inside the digits
and it will hold off enchantment for hours
until we reach the motel and sleep

what are the truths we honor about ourselves?
why do they never come to us in any strange hour
in any strange country
in any silence?

Two of Us Staring into Another Dimension

In their dimension the seagulls expand now
to fit the daytime sky
all powder-gray falling and crashing
and coming to life again
like drunken dots in our eyes

We stare as they deify themselves
in their falling and coming to life
they are detailed shapes of urgency
a code we can't understand

A magnet deep in the river draws them downward
a tiny watery volcano shoots them upward
they cringe and float and rear lightly out of reach
like dots in our eyes drunken with human love

If we could tear open those bodies and unwind
from them their fatal wild guts
would they tell us anything about ourselves?
why are they so safe from us?
they are the jerking soaring pinpoints of love
as near as we know to the shapes of love
safe in a dimension we can't understand

The Good Life Here on Earth

in love
we are drawn in a long curve
like the rising of light
across the photographed globe

in love
we taste other mouths
indifferent

original
in every earthly touch
in love we repeat motions
we repeat love
we repeat our rising of love
like the fierce scanning of light
across the moving earth

Growing Together

we have tangled together
too often
our sleep has tangled mossy and sinister
as old rocks
our faces pressed together in sleep
have taken on the slumber of rocks, rocks' faces,
which are the least important part
of rocks

the veins of your forehead have swollen
like vines
my hair has grown too long
down onto your chest
our toenails outlined in harmless old dirt
scrape against all our legs
for weeks

we have embraced
too often
our arms have tangled slick with sweat
like the sweat of oil on water
making phosphorescent
the swimmers and their innocent limbs
the glow shows them everywhere
no escape in any dark

rising, pulling back my long sweaty hair
I see a face in the mirror only half mine
what I am thinking is only half mine
these words are only half mine
the frayed threads of our bodies want
only that tangling again
that old growing together again
a completion like the exhaling
of a single breath

Giving Oneself a Form Again

My ribs are stuck too close together
the horizon is too close!
too close!
ground to a fine grim dust
the soul recalls an earlier shape
a child's shape
tough as stone
"Everything is too close!"

The child will not be touched

After the swift tearing of cloth
a woman recoils
to her earliest peace
the body has always been too close
too close the breathing of love

So she forms herself again
with her own hands
with a certain knowledge she strokes
the legs to calmness
like wasps the blood flares
and subsides
she forms again the thoughtful
altitude of thigh
forming again the face
the darting eyes
that see those iron spikes of fences
beside sidewalks of ice

Wounds

the pigment peels
from us
the total form of ourselves
falls from us

words elude
this music—
is it the sun breaking
into our private blood?

the sun breaks to delirium
my skin jumps
at its surface
what are the noises the raw air holds,
is it the Old Testament breaking loose?

my skin is rubbed raw
the pigment sucked out
you outline my face constantly
with your thumbs—
I am a wound nursed open
germless in the hot sun

        it is not a baptism
        or a fury from an old god's beak
        but an ordinary violence
        framed by windowsills
        the loosing of fresh blood
        an ordinary violence
        girls strain from windowsills
        to achieve

A Lover

the earth of public parks
frozen beneath litter
draws the body
relentlessly

the highest leaf is a sophistry
air and words drawn downward
asserted in perfection
downward

a molecule in the edge
of one's eye
expands to mystery

You are the child
not included in the class photograph
mysteriously you are missing
you bring the ship's mast
down with a joking blow
you don't wear gloves, a hat,
you don't mind the cold, my
coldness

drawn downward to perfection
drawn to a surface of small deadly cracks
I know that we are momentary
in our perfection
lost in the pace of your breathing
the perfection you are always imagining
drawing us downward
evasive of daylight
the body asserted in perfection
downward

Morning on Our Beach

bobbing, bouncing with the look
of being alive, three fish turn up
this morning, dead, glowing
like sour milk

so slippery the water can't
hold them!—bearded, bristled,
very hard and white, stomachs
sturdy with entrails!—look, they
are perfect fish

close in a flurry of minnows still
living, shapes brief and silly
as fingernails, swirl around the fish
and away: the fish are fatherly,
being dead

yesterday our navigators said
"the surface of the moon is tranquil"
down here the river sends us messages
of fat white fish
waves splash mutely in our heads
bringing our brains to float

though we own it to the ships' channel
the river is making faces

smiles break upon cries
frothy gums crossed by lips that look neuter
ah, the private beaches everywhere
are perplexed
how can we handle so much water?
daylight multiplies our three fish
our sand is littered with deader debris
multiplied are the two of us raking
on the surface of the earth

You / Your

you must be imagining walls:
my arms brush against them

your eyes are small hazy suns
      with the look of being blind
drawing me up to
day

if you were to turn me lightly
      inside out
I would become the fixed center
of the famous universe

Public Love

Listen, they are applauding.
The tops of their skulls—
cautious half-dollar-sized holes—
are showing through the earth.
The worm-fine soil about them
is agitated; we are doing well.

My love, we are on exhibit.
There is nothing private
in the senses.
Falling upon me you make me delicate,
a universal woman!
Others have done these things before.
A man like you has fallen
in an avalanche of love upon me
or upon someone like me.
Others have done these things before.
Most of them are now dead.

We rise suddenly as if called by name,
we have only been playing dead.
Where are our names? Who has seen us?
We are fine-grained and sweet and mild
now as apples, innocent of our bodies.

I think it is all those dead
lives in you I love,
dead men grown to roots
solid and loving in the earth,
holding down a new universe.
All the good husbands!
There is nothing deadly in their deaths.
Their golf-ball-sized eyes admire us.
We are loving in pantomime.

It is a scenario we have inherited.
It is an offering to what remains
of gods, their blood flowing into us,
their used-up love rising again
in our new bodies.

In Hot May

seeds shaped to dry wrinkled discs
are blown like crazy here
on my brick floor
their rampage is sharp and nearly invisible
wearing down the brick
they threaten
to turn into voices or trees or human men

the flood of seeds crackles
the start of white flame
seeds of trees enormous with distance
split and scarred and fat
with seed
dangerous about my bare feet

desirous of human skin
the seeds impale themselves
upon the warm wet surface
of female skin

The Struggle to Wake from Sleep

every morning I wake permanently
and then
I blow myself up like a balloon

I sense a zipper untracked
I sense the closets bulging with clothes
and piles of shoes to be sorted
    two by two

the day of my life fills itself out
like a balloon
sucking the breath from me
in moist red mouthfuls
I cross and recross the day's space
I have the hobbling humility
of an old man inching across a cafeteria floor

next door are boys trespassing
our absent neighbor's land
on the gusty river their fishing poles
make shadows
the black lines are slack, and taut
and violent with waves and the impatient
muscles of boys' young arms

all day I sort out clothes and containers of food
the day blows itself up slowly
my human head is stunned
that such mountains should go into it
       in long division
the boys' eyes construct columns
I am afraid of:
all day, wandering, strolling through my rooms
I feel the soft brushing of hooks
against my mouth

My Fate Met Me

at the bottom
of a week:
dazed from ordinary loss
of blood
I lay down before him
on the sidewalk
eyeballs hot and keen as bulbs
behind my translucent
female eyelids
the lids thin as lampshades of finest
light-emitting skin

women lose too much blood
and are then incompetent
of judgment
they become translucent
and see too much
seeing through their fine keen
skin:
a curse of an instinct

they lose blood enough
to write their names everywhere
initialing a city
in bright drying red

we meet our fates
pretending to feel pain
which we later feel
in truth
we tell lies and tell the truth
this is because our brains are weak
from loss of blood in our bodies
we feel blood seeping gently outward from us
and we meet our fates
often

Love and Its Derangements

They are always trying
to drag me by the hair, away

my skull prickles wisely
at the sound of their footsteps
they want to sink
into me the length of their
bodies   as into an enemy
with a sister's face

they want to learn from me
certain cries and names
they want the music rising to a shriek
they want the river's white sails
to collapse into the dirty water

always
the circular bones of their necks are alive
with desires unworded
always they lean their elbows onto tables
in a code of male conspiracy

they want the new grass
to suffocate beneath the newer seeds of trees
in a hot spring flood

in this hot May sun
the line is abrupt between male and female:
shadows of a million swinging leaves
across the inert grass

if I could turn outward
into the flat white walls
of the rooms we use
I would witness a body

at its fate tugged by the moon
all the inches of its skin
rubbed raw with the skin
of men

Breaking Apart

are the marvels of the body
hoarded somewhere, permanent and in detail
as dreams lovingly censored?

where are the days of the week?

we gathered speed these last months
like a moving van
rushing downhill—
what was left of our lives bumping together
out of control
inside that shell—

we developed the habit of checking
watches, checking time,
time being suddenly important
I did not trust your watch
you seemed not to trust mine
moving our wrists together was a gesture
we didn't know enough
to admire

the souls in our two bodies
have now been digested

Mysterious Motions
Subside

a woman comes to rest
enthralled to perfect stillness
a cupful of blood in her heart

the air contracts slowly about her
as about public monuments
famous and invisible

How people fall in love!
minds like moths
beating slowly like moths

love passes through her
on its way through her
mysterious motions subside
and become again flesh

Love Picnic

There are flies buzzing above the tables.
The trash can is overturned.
Pollen is yellow on our twenty fingers
    as we lie on our backs in the grass
    and decipher clouds.

Our fortune must descend upon us
    from clouds.

Fingernails, toenails, and hairs grow
faithfully, after death.
After love's death my stomach grows.
We while away decades yawning in the grass:
    "The ice is all melted"
    "The radio station is faded"
    "My skin is peeling away"

Love is smeared yellow on our fingers.
Experimentally we sniff our fingers, but
no smell.

Oh, the decade clouds over
with clouds of marvelous shapes!

Kids from another picnic crash through—
"Sorry about that!"
Years pass idly in this picnic.
In the eclipse of the moon we sat up
excited
and you fastened your lips to mine.
Love leapt like electricity between us.
It fell away.
The ground is friendly and absorbed your love
    like pop.

Now a radio is singing:
  "The ice is all melted"
  "The radio station is faded"
  "My skin is peeling away"

Passing an Afternoon

Blood transforms the warm bath water
and, in it, I see weakly
that this was a mistake.
The razor's cut is not deep, nevertheless
the blood rushes out happily in the warm
water as if kin to it, the same
tender substance.

Rising
a new person
transformed with an icy
sense of error
I go to the sink and turn on cold water
which is not friendly to blood.
The cut is deeper than imagined.
It hurts.

Splashes on the pale gold tile,
bright red bursts like sunlight,
like exclamation points—*Another error!*
I wrap a small towel around my wrist.
A small towel indicates a small error.

Soaked through
the towel's gold is tarnished.
There is an innocent joy in the blood's
flow that the towel and I cannot absorb.
These spurts, worth twenty dollars a pint
on the market, sense themselves unmarketable now.

Another towel wrapped tight in terror
slows everything down. On a blue velvet
love seat from which love has wandered I
sit waiting. I am an angel with an alert
backbone. I am purified from the business
of panic.

What I Fear . . .

What I fear is our sleeplessness
when we are alone
together—

Constantly we watch, our minds
drum, imaginary teeth
sink into our muscles.

We hear someone walking solidly
nearby, always the sounds of ordinary
unloving people nearby, in health.

How it is others sleep, lovers
in other bodies, dropping gently
to sleep in one bed?

In the silence after love
we are newly derailed and newly
awakened. If there is a radiance in us
it is only for others to see.

Drownings

No use to touch the face
of that object.
No use the bumping
of heads.
My words flutter in your
silence—all is sucked up—
all propelled into your blood.

The awful thing about drowning
is that you have so long
to regret your mistake—
drowning in someone's veins
or in the ordinary river,
propelled downstream.

> Drownings!—deaths on the river!
> A body dragged out this morning
> beneath the bridge excites a crowd
> of kids and a few old men standing
> without purpose on the banks.
> People like us look away, ashamed.
> The water creates monsters of dark
> heavy flesh and faces become
> unreadable.

Your body, too, is heavy with mysteries.
If I raise your hand to my face
I feel the sudden illumination
of all our bones
and I am ashamed.

After Love a Formal
Feeling Comes

pursued, I lie down flat
embraced, it is like a shot
of five o'clock traffic

oh I am pierced to my heart
every time
but then I fill in again
as if with glue

I evaporate and condense again
firm as tiny beads
of frost

reduced to a cage
of ribs and a smile
locked between my jaws
lie down flat again
being immortal

Jigsaw Puzzle

You have broken me up into pieces.
Chunks of flesh hand-sized
and bite-sized have fallen from
one another in surprise.
Look, they are pulsing.
You have broken me up into jigsaw
puzzle pieces.
They don't lie flat but are smeared everywhere
on the walls and ceiling and floor of this
room and in the air of this room
which we do not own.

All this mess, this bleeding
of puzzle parts, will have to
be cleaned up.
The parts must be forced back together.
They must add up to the shape
of a woman, a topographical map,
with proper directions of North and South.

American Expressway

the haze opens
and shuts stinging the eye
the picnic of wheels breaks

and closes again
the passing of bright cars
breaks in a music
    and shutters again

and again

5:30 PM
Detroit empties out
men's knuckles close with love
    on their steady steering wheels
traffic rises familiar and conversational
seams in the roadway are melting

the pulse of the dance is discernible
in the lower backbone
the speedometer needle rises
    and pauses
and rises white and firm again
the breaths of engines are humid

tonight the expressway will be relived in sleep
in the sleep of its constant drivers
relived with the repetition of love

but now

the column stops
now the vessels giddy with motion are braked
    but cannot stop
"Don't touch me!" cry the radios
the cars' sheen like birds' slick feathers:

"Don't touch me, not me!"
the column adds itself up rapidly like numbers
    like magic

explosion far in the rear
a shuddering of fingertips
and readable now on the pavement are designs
of oil and gas and blood
out to the very edge where
the old weeds live
the windshield pops
the safety glass flies backward
into an open mouth

the door flies open like magic
like automation!
we spit out bits of glass
    like used-up teeth
ah, the time is now 5:31 PM

a cop is noting this time

humid and hot and mild is the dream
the expressway's smog lifting
lowering

    the smog lifts
lowers like sleep

hobbling to the side we press
cloth darkening against the gash
our hands are prickly with bits of glass
one eye has come loose

sitting
on the oily grass at the edge

we are like cameras recording speeders
we grin out at the parade of cars
old friends emptying out of the city

the afternoon buzzes
Detroit is emptying out
vessels gleaming and solid in a dream
unhurrying at seventy miles an hour
at 5:32 PM
the column reassembles itself like a backbone
of detachable vertebrae

Disintegration

We who tell lies look
through the dictionary, looking
for words that are true.
Unsordid in truth such words
must exist: we have heard of them.

We in love skate
over the knuckles of others.
They say, "Why did you do that?"
We reply, "We are accomplishing certain
difficult turns."

The pond glimmers in winter with
powdery threads and cracks of
lies, a pattern that was once
beautiful, but we went on
too long. We in love

go on too long, carried by momentum.
Our words in momentum keep on
practiced in agility, with lies.
Benjamin Franklin said
Games lubricate the body and the mind.

Don't You Know the Private Life Is Over?

Purity in the columns
a rigid unsurprise
when the newsprint
smears
it will reassert itself
in the margins
private purity of thumb
whorled fingerprints
the calculus of absolute
fate

When she rose that day
the type was being cleaned
for her story
clocks moved in unison
in her kitchen and in vast rooms
of printing presses
her face now is pretty
but the urgency of its
atoms is stilled . . . .
the picture is made of tiny
dots of newsprint
not atoms

Permanently she smiles
unsensational
to that photographer
(graduation from secretarial
school, 1967) unsensational in
the shock of a second's light
her head is no longer
on her shoulders
processed out of sight
she is tagged

shaken in test tubes
evidence is being collected
with tweezers

The face continues
its smiling between columns
of serious print
the stilled dots of atoms
held to the light
reveal contrary dots
on the opposite page
anti-selves
anti-fate
another photograph
another smile of perpetual
unsurprise

Madness
for Scott C.

threatened by their integrity
we contemplate the mad
as they contemplate
their madness

no alteration
in them no unfaithfulness
no scattering and rearranging
of love—

they are faithful as crippled lovers
basking in institutional sunlight
uncaged but faithful
to their cages

their dreaming skulls
shake out nets for us
their voices trickle
between our ribs

if we knew them
as relatives, or friends
now they are unknowable
and sacred

their eyes
leap into our faces

Portrait

There the face is growing.
No part permanently shaped
but growing out of strange raw colors—
turpentine wash—
the eyes molecules that do not see me
and are wise with being immortal.

Here, I sit by the window.
In the big mirror behind the painter
I can see the face growing, my face
growing free of me—
it is floating free of me in the room
somewhere between the artist's darting mind
and my body.
My fate is outside me and I am afraid.

Shaped to the canvas in sure relentless strokes
it is myself being born from me,
the surface of myself peeled from me,
the facial skin reclaimed for that canvas.
The mystery of all our faces is here!—
I think they are sinister and lovely,
growing over our blunt bones.

That is a face more delicate than the one
I would claim. It does not even breathe.
Light feeds it; small shots of lightning in the skin.
Beneath the harsh brush the pores
do not need to breathe, the eyes will never
close, the lips have nothing to declare.
It is at peace, being immortal.
It is a terrible fact.
I see how the fact of myself is a puzzle of parts
forced into a certain shape,
a tiny void filling an ordinary canvas.

Mirage
for Patricia Hill Burnett

what is the burden of that flesh?
unreadable the design of your being
behind the platitude of eyes
the lazy alluring tendrils of your soul

beauty at the surface of your being
stretched to acclaim upon the ancient bones' design
and unreachable from inside
unreadable even to you

there is nothing ordinary in you
except the maplike structure of your insides
while on the outside you excite
images in eyes that will be soured
as they wake to ordinary days

this is preposterous to you:
the burden of your flesh
and the furrowed dreams you raise
in faces you cannot accommodate
this is a curse upon you:
the dance they expect you to dance
until the muscles of your comely limbs
ache with their years of toil
in that womanly frame—

men have no idea of your body
they do not see the body
they see only the dance of the body in its toil
its perspiring circles and convulsions
in a service of dreaming
beneath the golden cloth such women wear
to cover their bones' design

Diving

like applause
the roar in the ears—
the fast, fast tendrils of air
blasted to water—
the surface looked tranquil enough
to sleep upon
but it is a storm
inside itself

I dive and you dive beside me
my eyes are sharply closed
shot back up into the air
as if unwanted by the river's mud
I snap my eyes open
unblinded
wondering where will I come
to life this time?

you emerge beside me noisily
water shakes from us onto us
one or the other of us will
seize a hand
someone's fingers will stroke
someone's lush running skin

we are always diving and returning
back to life again as if born
with the same bodies again
the same faces
always the same storm takes us
and casts us back up

Love and Time

after that second of clarity
the awful shock of love
the wheels and jewels of my watch
work minutely

dreaming, the tiny watch face
outdreams all its seconds
there are gold dots for numbers
time is abbreviated and chaste

a strand of hair in my mouth—
pupils of my eyes like dots, blind
with the abrupt sadness of love—
my face stiffens into a dream

below, the torn flower of my body
perspiration a luminous haze
everything female and intricate
like a watch's expensive perfection

The Secret of the Water
Off Point Pelee

Ohio's shore is out of sight today and
the lake is therefore infinite.
We are standing cold in the waves
staring at the waves breaking
about our soft stomachs.
What is this din in the air?

Fish are flopping onto the hot sand
whitely like rubber fish. We are
swimming in white foam. We are
rocked by the happy spasms of
our bodies' muscles. What a cataclysm
of seagulls and fish and human
arms and heads!

In this infinite lake you encircle me
with your arms loving like the water,
intimate down to the pores
of your skin. I see the crease of untanned flesh
at your throat—with your cold lips you suck
these old, old freckles on my shoulder.
The waves knock us apart.

We struggle back together again.
We collide. Our lungs are pumping like
arms and legs—we will stay afloat!
nostrils clean and clear of this water!
Very cold is the side of your face, my love,
your loving skull.
The air gasps around us.

Waves fight and ebb and fight again.
There are shouts of children and airplanes
in another windy element

and waves and our pumping lungs that celebrate
what is left of us—alive, in love, in this
crashing water off Point Pelee—
We have not gone down today.

Ordinary Summer Days

bugs are stamped out briskly
by men's large fists
wicker chairs unspring
unfocused are rose petals
someone has snapped with his fingers

everything shifts
   gradually out of focus
the banana stamped 29¢ turns brown
small comets collide in the eye

elm seeds flutter in old cobwebs
sand dries salty on our feet
broken combs, broken glass, broken shoes
wash up on shore
strangers' gifts disguised as debris

in summer the sun moves defiant
our shoulders blister and peel
our contorted shadows have no past
   nothing stays
the X of our lives' center
does not stay but shifts
   gradually out of focus

my body is solid and helpless
beneath the trivia of summer
it feels the days flow upward
its spectacular exploding cells
   flowing upward
each cell a special fate!—
yet flowing upward like seeds
like dried dead bugs caught in the wind
like skin flaking from shoulders
in a cold afternoon in July

"I don't like for people to scream at me 'cause all I do is holler back"

body by singular body they give no sign
of being crucial
but the institution wise with danger
has 1,550 locks

a girl with dark sweaty skin
a man's socks
a mess of fourteen years
"if we get that far not being caught
then they take us in"—
knowing the rooms where children
who are girls might hide

but here opulence of tile, white
raw germless scent of disinfect
here are young citizens just
deloused
a telephone rings forever in the distance
their eyes dart without knowledge

the attendants sell them pills
flat on the tongue
a needle is always for rent somewhere
the children's detention bursts
with razor-sharp flashes of light

some break out
others break in
outside, waiting
are children waiting for locks to unlock
"Let us in" they cry to playgrounds
of concrete and wire fences
they imagine the cots   the running water

they are children huddled beneath stairs
or at dumps' fires
waiting

Landscapes

I. A LANDSCAPE OF BACK YARDS

The train's approach is abrupt and sly
the back yards are never prepared
there are back windows of back rooms
there are back porches with garbage cans
the backs of garages filled with junk
for five minutes we stare into the back
of someone's life: a woman is dreaming
busily in a kitchen

We have finished the New York Times
the pages are smudged forever
our fingers are smudged
we stare into the back of a lighted kitchen
where a man's shape has now appeared
the woman at the window gives no sign
she must be working
over a sink
the train jerks and she gives no sign
of seeing   her shoulders and head still
the back door opens and the man appears
he stares out at us
across a small continent of blackness
a yard backwards and square
a patch of frozen domestic muck
what remains of cornstalks in winter

the man rubs his hands together
without meaning

The train jerks and pulls away
we think at once: our love
will be articulate

always fixed to a certain shape
no one will examine it at random
we sit this evening on the train's dirty seats
in a used compartment of the train
our feet on the *New York Times*
our faces frozen to this time

II. A LANDSCAPE OF FORMS

The absolute center of any structure
though invisible
draws the eye as if
the eye were swinging from a string

The enormous flower of a thought
inside a stationary body
inside a stationary building
is an event of terror

Blocks of concrete united to an empire—
the hesitant cracks of human walls—
the final shape of a building is a fall
from a pinnacle someone has dreamt

Such etiquette in the meeting of walls!
firmly fixed are floors and ceilings
and girders in their places invisible
beneath carpeting courteous to the feet

A few thousand cubic feet of air
contain the events of any room
without terror the rectangle remains itself
all unholiness remains eternally itself

Being holy we come upon in the darkness
of any room the remains of someone's joy
a holy flowering in someone's brain
we think *These doors will not be our true exits.*

III. A LANDSCAPE OF LOVE

They do not believe in the horizon of rooms
like the notes of Bach that run through the mind
their hair and fingers are always
spilling together

it is an explosion of sounds
notes that would never know themselves
separate
        separated

they do not believe in the oneness of a self
they have felt their skins
slough off all horizons
the walls of rooms rear away from them
and the birds in any wallpaper are golden and still
in reverence

it is their privilege to think *I am someone who is loved*

Love is a matter of words being aired
it is a matter of the choice of words
that, being aerated, shape a world

How Gentle

how gentle are we rising
easy as eyes in sockets turning

intimate the hardness: jaw
upon jaw, forehead warm

upon forehead
kisses like breaths, involuntary

love: I am illuminated
in and out of love's breathing

fluorescent glowing the fine
warm veins and bones

your weight is
the sky lowered suddenly

I am loved: a message
clanging of a bell in silence

you are heavy with surprise
the horizon surrenders

are we wearing out
our skins' defenses?

turning to silk, texture of flashy
airy surfaces scant as breaths?

I am loved: the noon slides gently
suddenly upon us to wake us